Instructional Fair's *Geometry–Grade 2* is a different way for children to learn about geometry. This book focuses on experimenting with shapes and spatial relationships, not just on learning the names of shapes. While doing puzzles and completing patterns, children are developing problem-solving and organizing skills.

Geometry has often been neglected in elementary schools, but recently many educators have been recommending much more geometry content. They believe geometry is useful in a variety of ways in life and that it can also be another context for teaching children problem solving, logic, organizing, and other thinking skills.

Children will differ in their home experiences with geometry and in their innate ability to understand spatial relationships. Some children will have played with puzzles and blocks at home. Others will have had few such experiences. Some children will have a head start on others simply because seeing shapes is something at which they are inherently good. Interestingly enough, children who are good with numbers are not necessarily good with shapes, and children who have trouble with the abstract nature of numbers may find shapes much more concrete and understandable.

As you use the pages in this book with your students, you will find some students will do well on their own, and others will need extra help. Having children work with partners helps. Sharing and discussing the students' results as a class can also help. You may need to try some of the puzzles ahead of time or along with your students.

The geometric skills in this book are grouped by type of activity. The activities are presented in order of difficulty, but their difficulty will vary from child to child. The book is divided into sections, starting with math facts involving shapes and then offering activities on finding shapes, shading shapes, puzzles with cutout pieces, drawing shapes, making designs, patterns, coloring designs, and folding puzzles. The directions on the pages may need to be read aloud and discussed. A glimpse at the answer key may help you better understand the intent of a page. (Note: When children are asked to "shade" a shape, they should use a pencil.) Some children may need help with the cutting and folding.

Geometry–Grade 2 should be motivating and exciting for children. Rather than using the pages all together as a unit, you might want to consider using one or two a week throughout the year as a change of pace from arithmetic. However you use them, you will find yourself enjoying them right along with your students!

Hidden Sums

Name_____

♦ Shade in each shape with the correct sum. The first one is done for you.

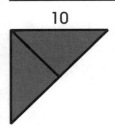

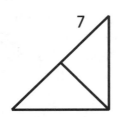

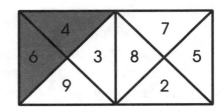

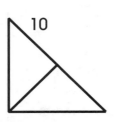

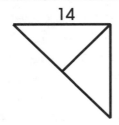

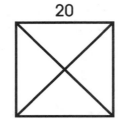

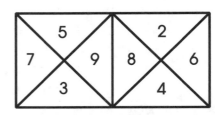

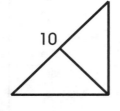

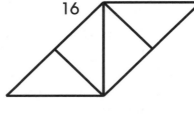

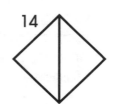

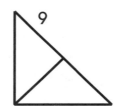

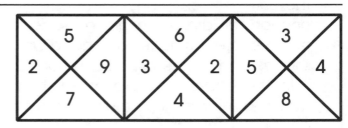

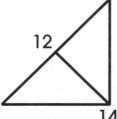

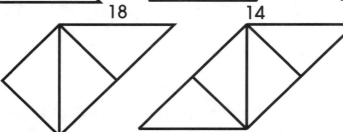

More Hidden Sums

Name_____

- ♦ Find the shape with the correct sum.
- ♦ Copy the numbers that make that sum. The first one is done for you.

11

3
8

12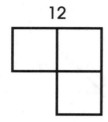

24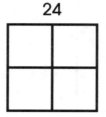

20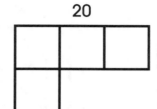

5	6	3	7
9	4	8	2

17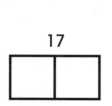

18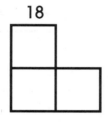

22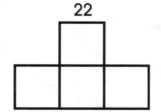

25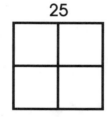

4	7	3	5
6	2	9	8

13

18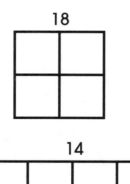

20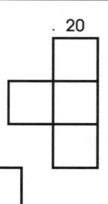

14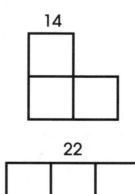

5	8	2	4
3	7	9	6
3	5	2	4

14

22

7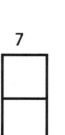

17

13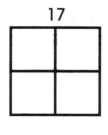

20

23

3	9	5	2
6	4	8	7
5	3	2	4

IF5126 Geometry Grade 2

Hidden Differences

Name_____

◆ Find the shape with the correct difference.
◆ Copy the numbers that make that difference. The first one is done for you.

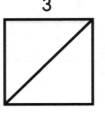
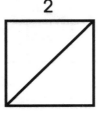
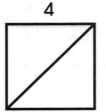

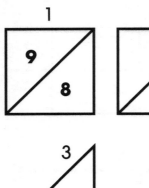

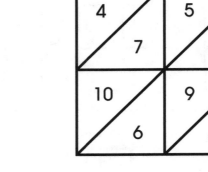

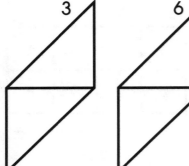

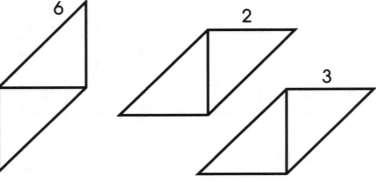

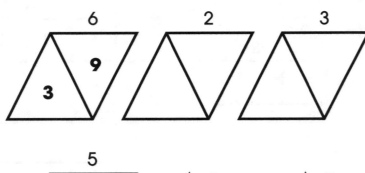

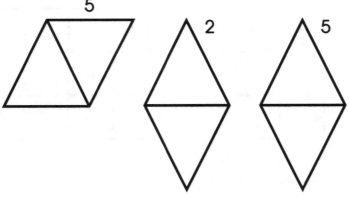

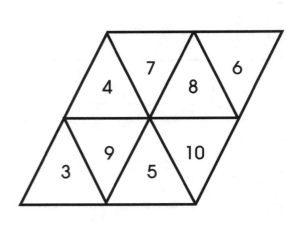

More Hidden Differences

Name_____

♦ Find the shape with the correct difference.
♦ Copy the numbers that make that difference. The first one is done for you.

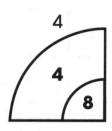

4

4
8

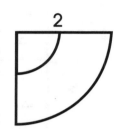

2

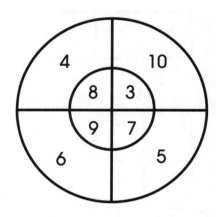

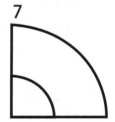

7

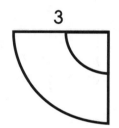

3

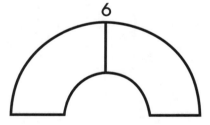

6

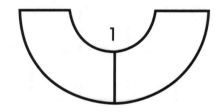

1

2   5

2

4

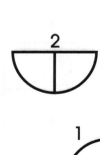

1

5

5

Lots of Hidden Sums   Name_____

- ◆ Find the shape with the correct sum.
- ◆ Copy the numbers under the sum. The first one is done for you.

14

3	**1**	**10**

14

11

3	4	1	8
7	5	6	4
2	9	2	6
5	3	1	10

22

9

16

18

20

16

21

18

25

21

6

Discover the Design

Name_____

♦ Each shape can be found in the rectangles below. Shade in Shape 1 in Rectangle 1 at the bottom of the page. Do the same for all the others.

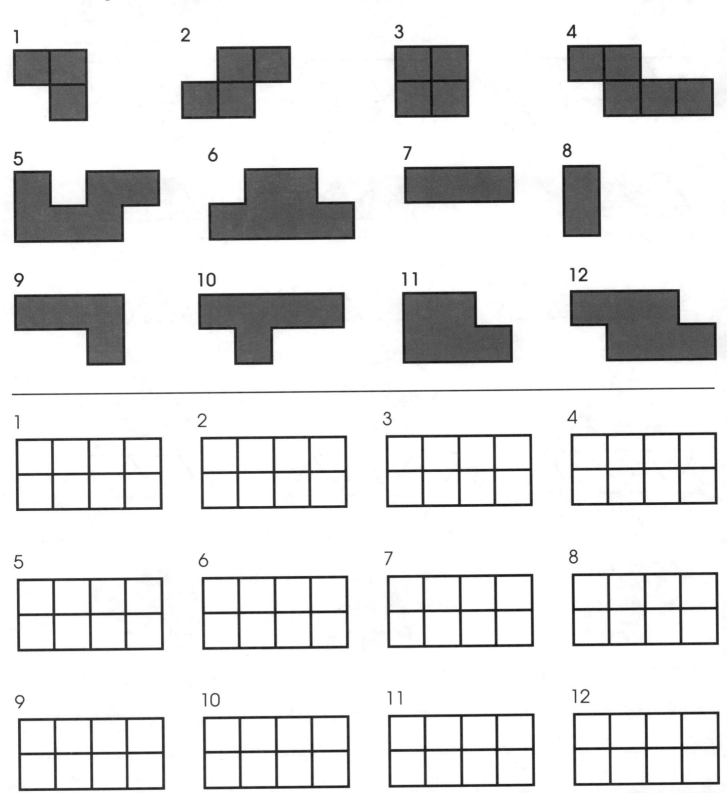

Hidden Shapes

Name_____

◆ Shade each shape in the design below it.

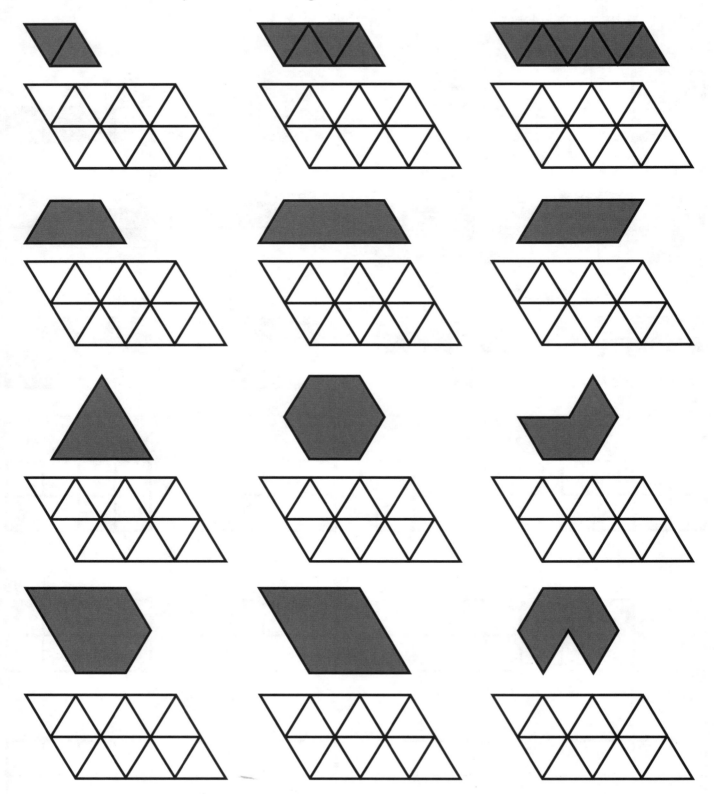

Find the Shapes

Name_____

♦ Shade each shape in the design below it.

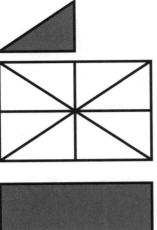 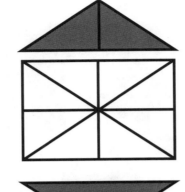 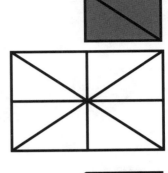

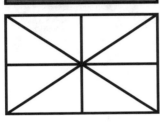 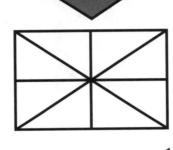 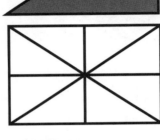

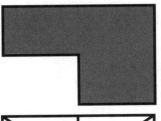 

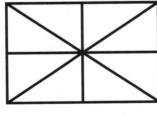 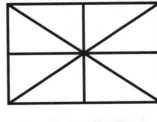 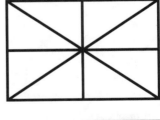

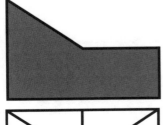  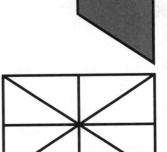

Triangle Shapes

Name _____

◆ Shade each shape in the triangle design below. You may need an extra copy of the triangle design.

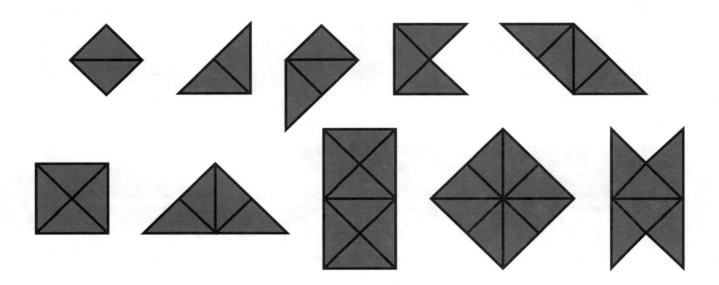

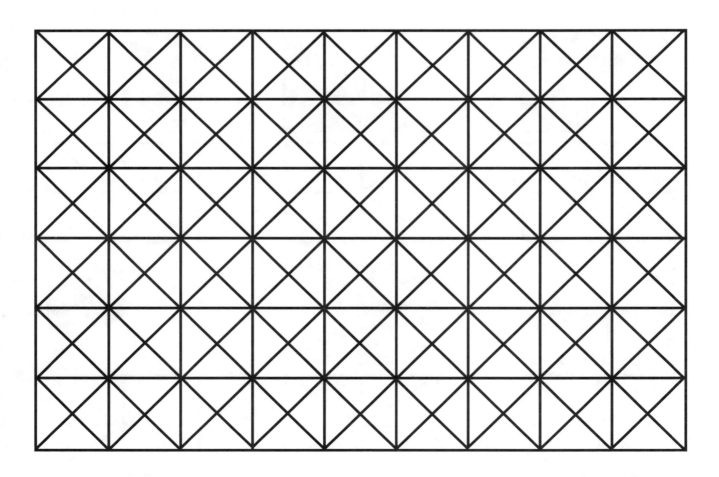

Zigzag Shapes

Name_____

◆ Shade each shape in the design below. You may need an extra copy of the design.

Rectangles in Hiding

Name_____

♦ Shade a different rectangle in each design. Squares do not count.

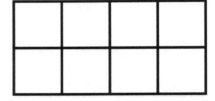

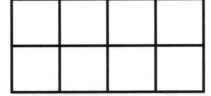

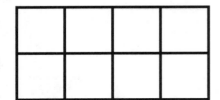

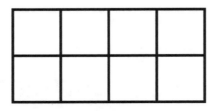

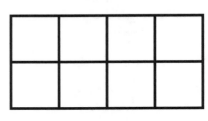

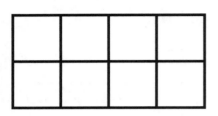

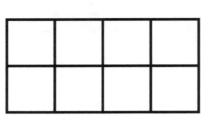

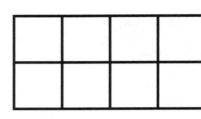

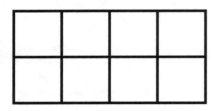

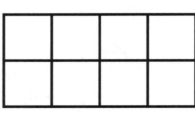

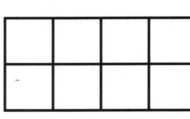

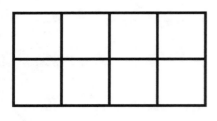

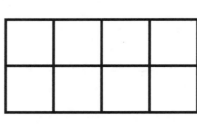

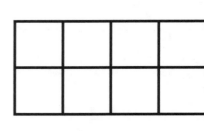

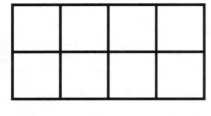

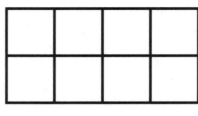

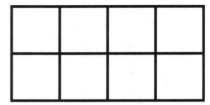

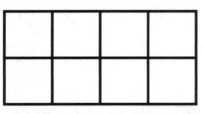

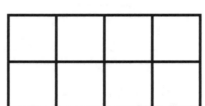

Did you find all 19?
If not, keep trying!

Four Triangle Shapes   Name⎯⎯⎯⎯⎯⎯⎯⎯⎯

◆ Shade 4 triangles in each design to make a different shape.

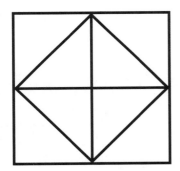 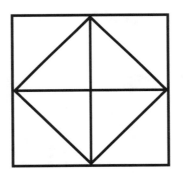 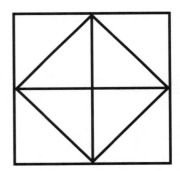

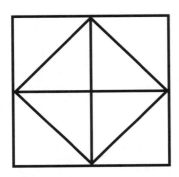 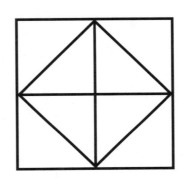 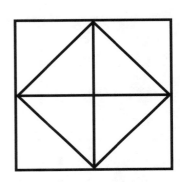

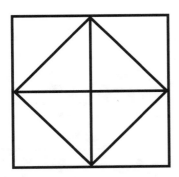 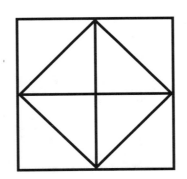 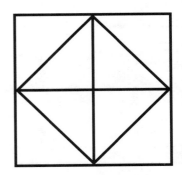

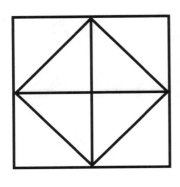 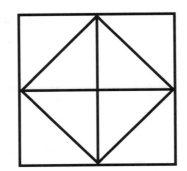 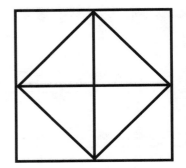

Squzzles

Name_____

- ◆ Cut out all the "A" pieces on the next page.
- ◆ Put them on Squzzle A so they fit the outline.
- ◆ Do the same for Squzzles B, C and D.

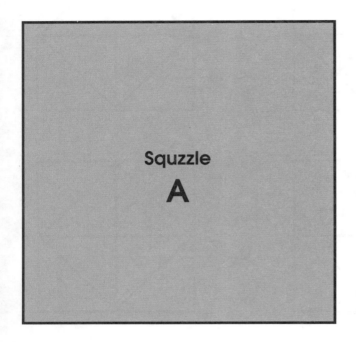

Squzzle
A

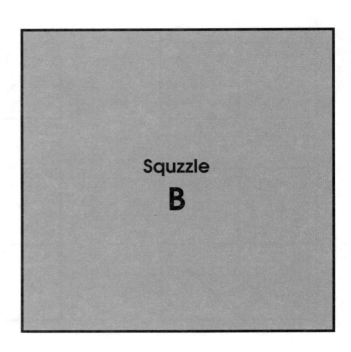

Squzzle
B

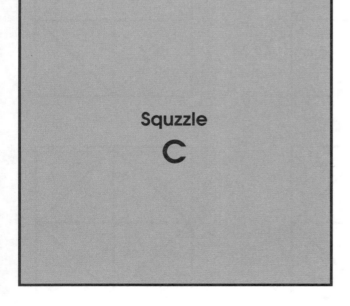

Squzzle
C

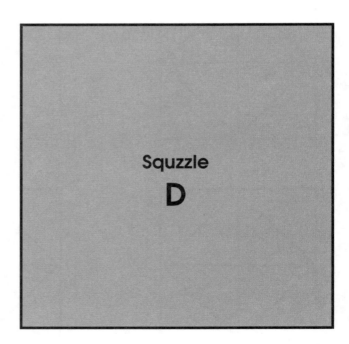

Squzzle
D

Squzzles

Name_____

♦ Use with page 14.

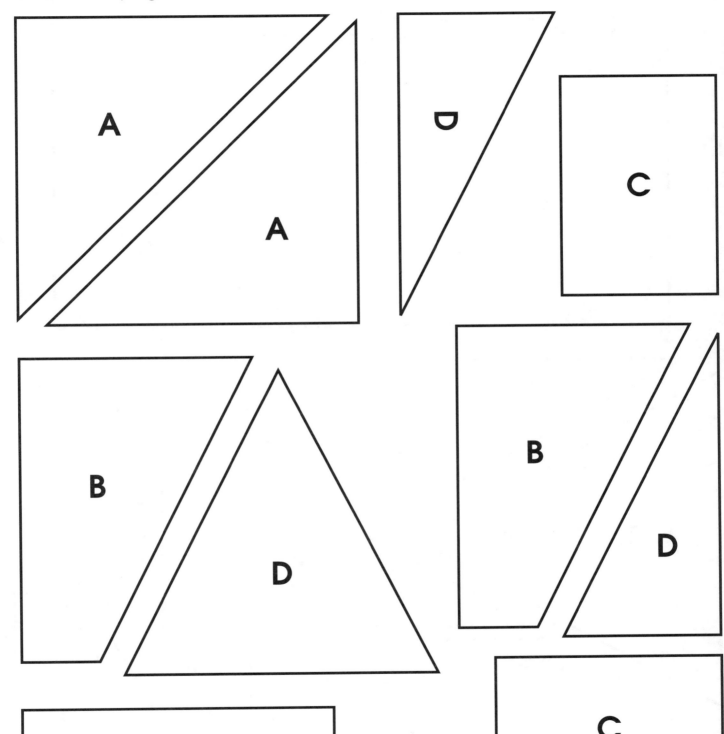

Rectuzzle 1

Name_____

◆ Cut out all the "1" pieces below.
◆ Put them on this Rectuzzle so they fit the outline.

Rectuzzle

1

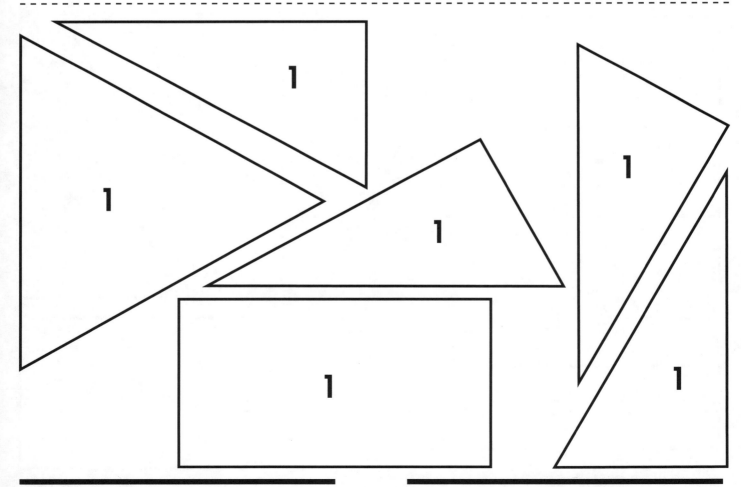

More Rectuzzles

Name_____

♦ Cut out the "2" pieces on page 18. Put them on Rectuzzle 2 so they fit the outline. Do the same for Rectuzzles 3, 4 and 5.

Rectuzzle
2

Rectuzzle
3

Rectuzzle
4

Rectuzzle
5

Rectuzzle Pieces

Name_____

♦ Use with page 17.

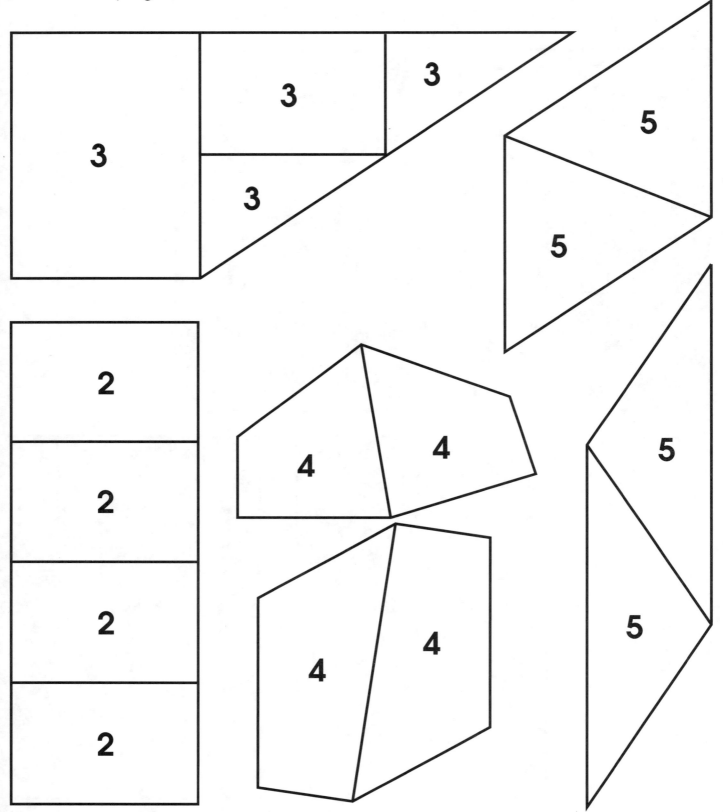

Trianguzzles

Name_____

- ◆ Cut out all the "A" pieces on the next page. Put them on Trianguzzle A so they fit the outline.
- ◆ Do the same for Trianguzzles B and C.

**Trianguzzle
A**

**Trianguzzle
B**

**Trianguzzle
C**

Trianguzzle Pieces

Name_____

♦ Use with page 19.

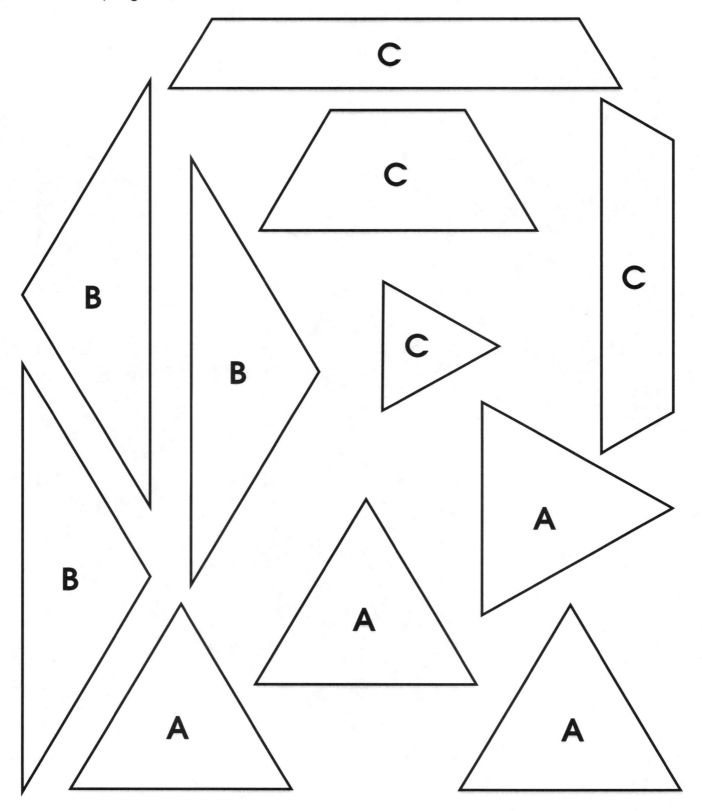

Circle Puzzles

Name_____

♦ Cut out the 4 pieces of the circle. Use them to make each shape.

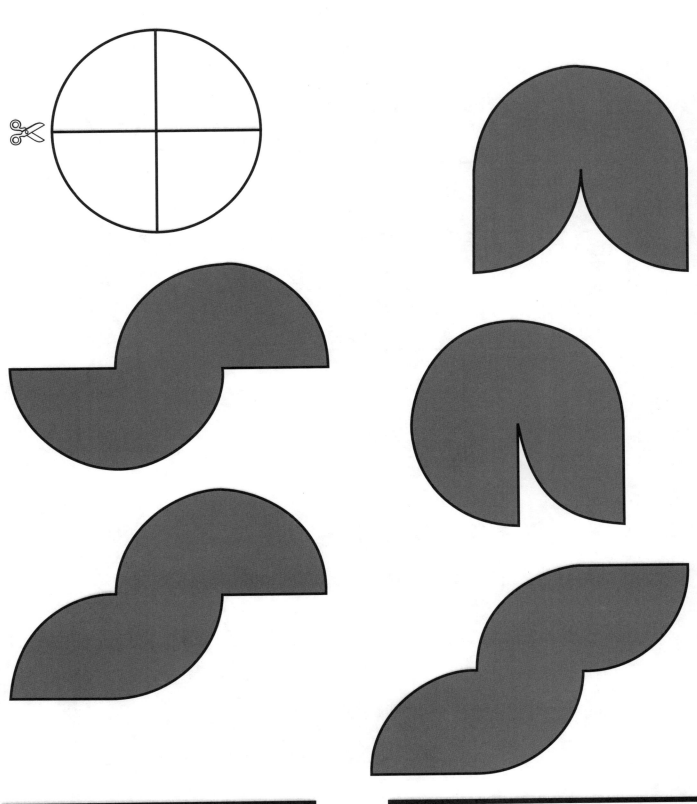

XYZ Puzzle

Name _____

- ◆ Cut out pieces X, Y and Z.
- ◆ Make each shape below using all 3 pieces.

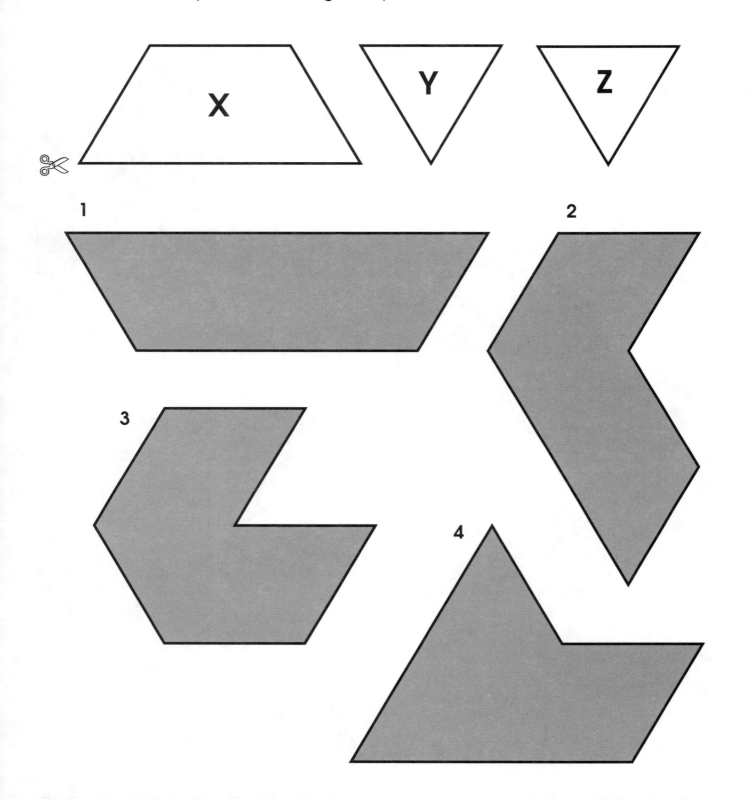

The Two Triangles

Name_____

- ♦ Cut out the 2 triangles at the bottom of the page.
- ♦ Make a shape like each below only larger. Use both triangles for each shape. You might have to flip a triangle.

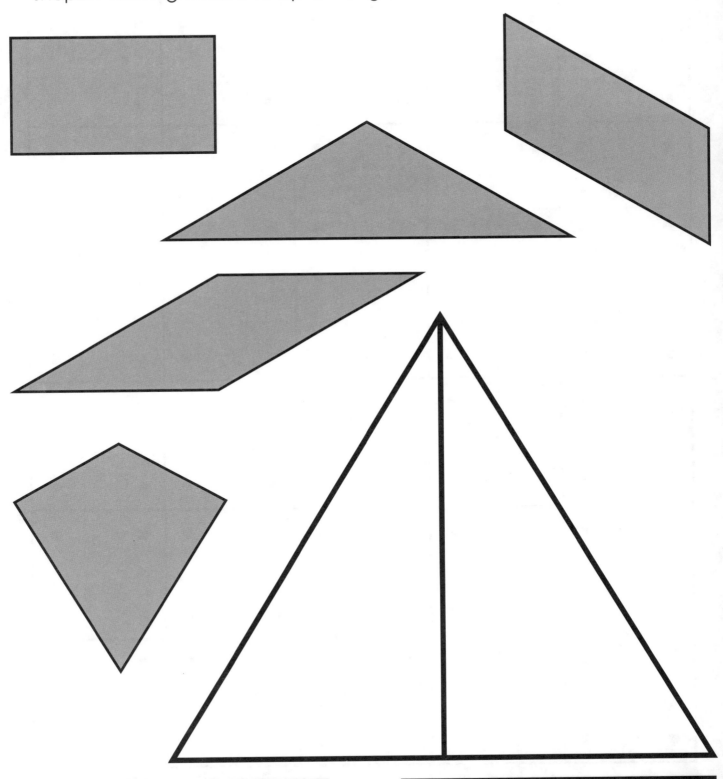

Dot Figures

Name_____

♦ Connect some dots in each box using from 1 to 6 lines.
♦ See how many different figures you can make.

Dots and Shapes

Name_____

♦ Connect dots to make each shape described.

Make a square.

Make a rectangle.

Make a 4-sider.

Make a different
4-sider.

Make a triangle.

Make a different
triangle.

Make a different
triangle.

Make a different
triangle.

Make a design.

Hexagon Patterns

Name_____

◆ Shade triangles in each design to make a different shape.

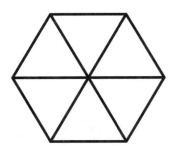

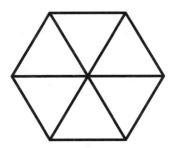
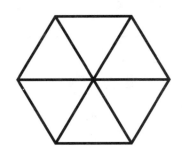

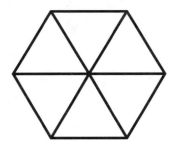

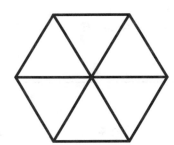

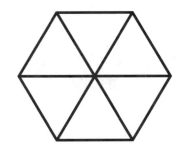

IF5126 Geometry Grade 2

Triangle Designs

Name_____

♦ Shade triangles in each design to make a different shape.

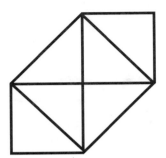 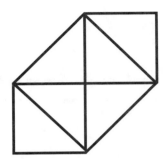 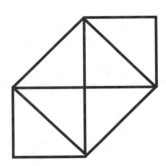

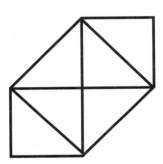 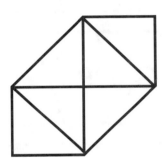 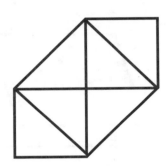

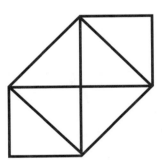 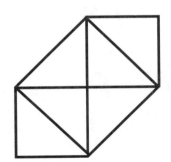 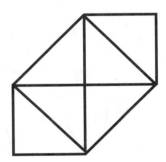

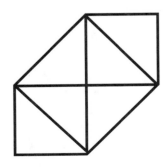 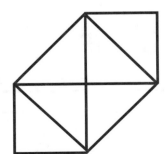 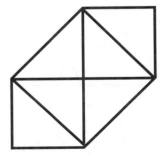

Coloring Patterns

Name_____

♦ Use green and blue crayons.
♦ Color the shapes with letters. Then color to keep the pattern going.

G	B	G	B					
green	blue	green	blue					

B	G	G	B	G	G			

G	B		G	B				

G		B		G				

B	B	G	B	B	G			

G	G	G	B	B	B			

B	B		B	B				

Square Patterns

Name _____

♦ Shade to keep each pattern going.

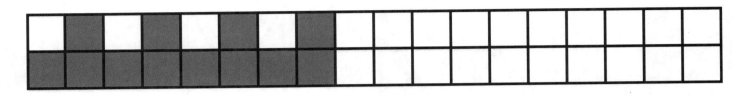

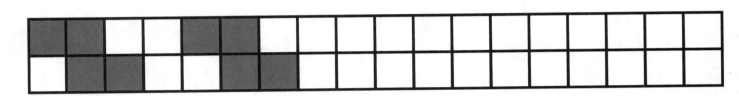

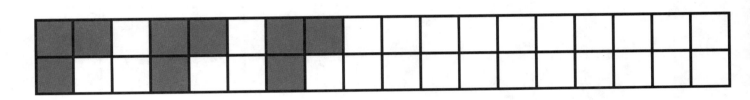

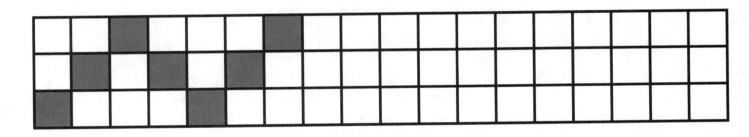

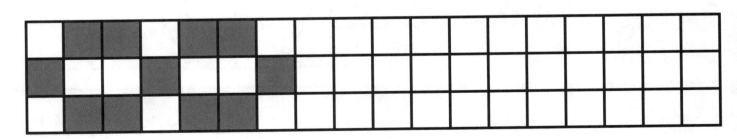

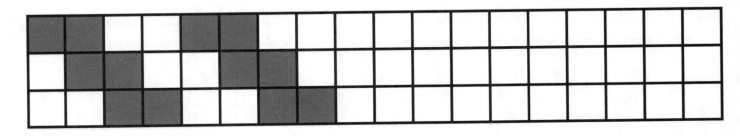

© Instructional Fair, Inc.   IF5126 Geometry Grade 2

Triangle and Rectangle Patterns

Name _____

♦ Shade to keep each pattern going.

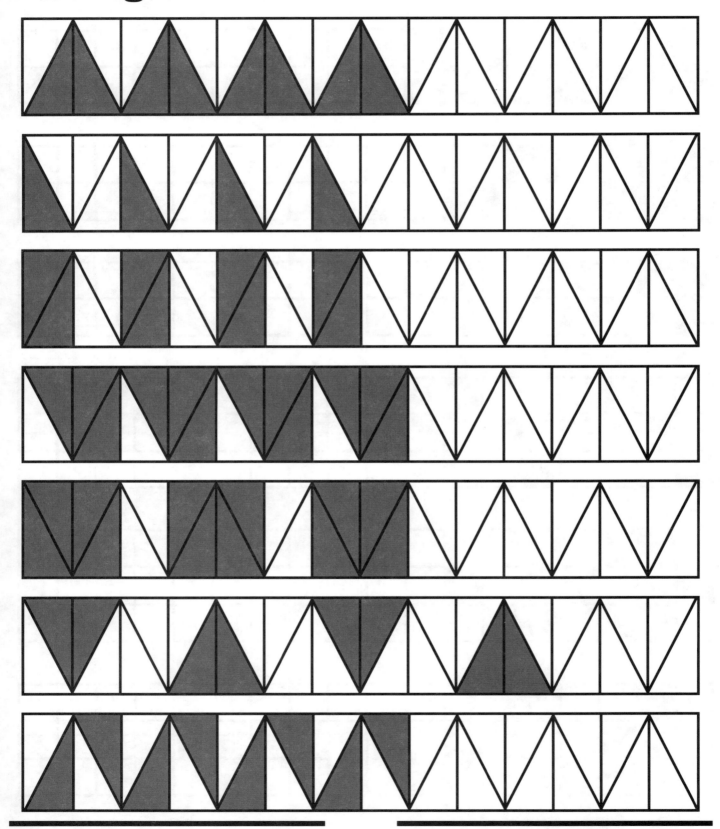

Triangle Patterns

Name_____

♦ Shade to keep each pattern going.

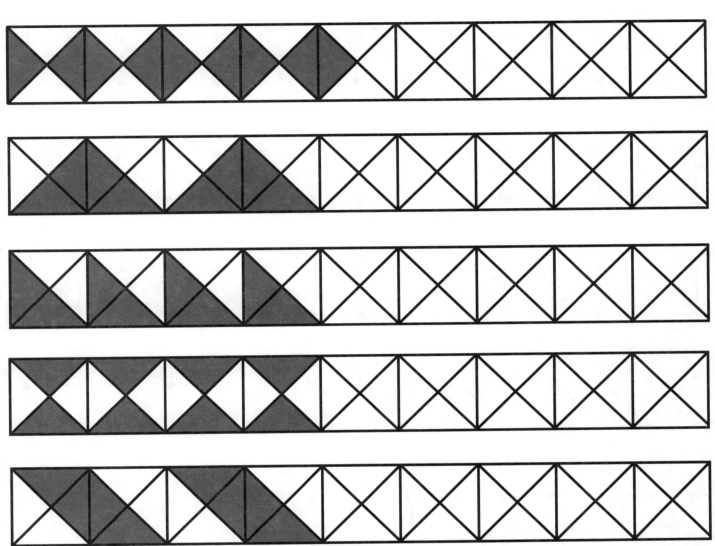

♦ Make your own patterns.

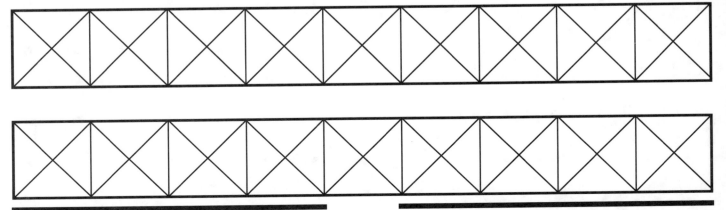

31

Dot Patterns

Name_____

♦ Connect the dots in each row to keep each pattern going.

Square in Rows

◆ Shade to keep each pattern going.

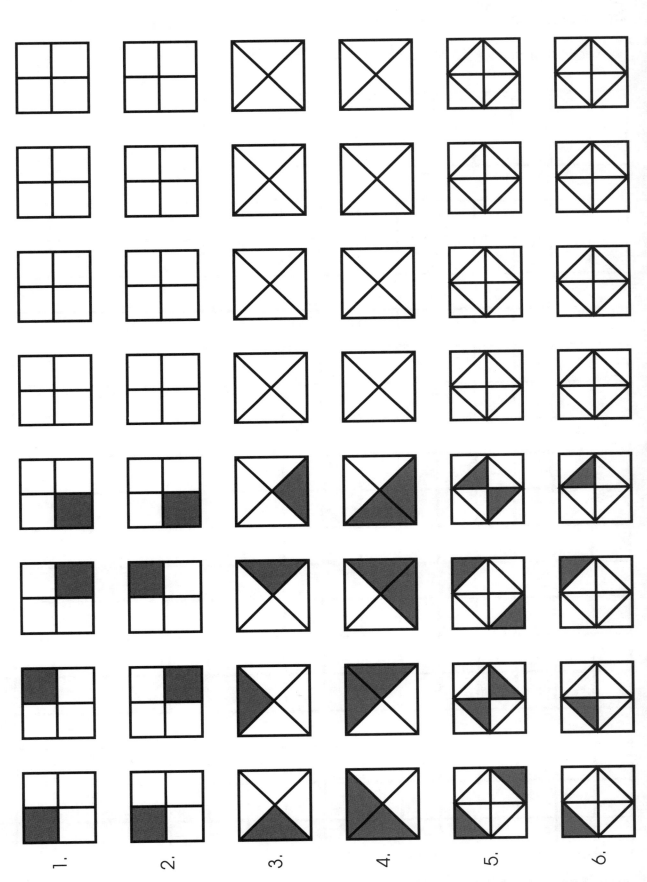

1.
2.
3.
4.
5.
6.

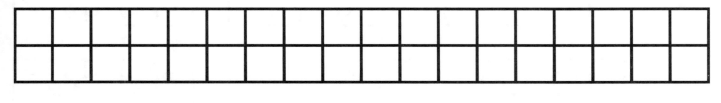

Square Patterns

Name_____

♦ Color or shade each design in a different pattern.

Triangle Patterns

◆ Using 1 crayon, color to make a different pattern in each row.

Name

35

Wallpaper Patterns

Name_____

♦ Shade to keep each wallpaper pattern going.

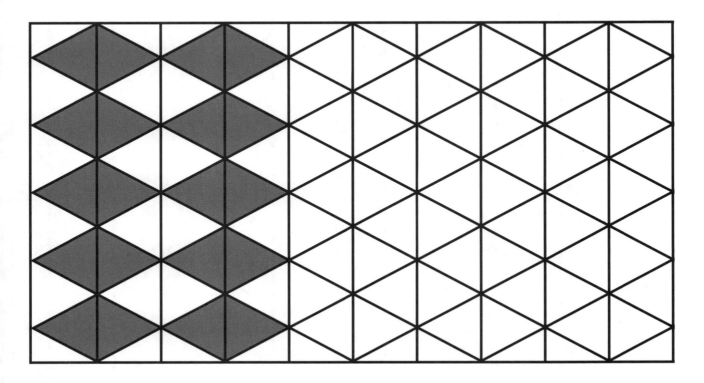

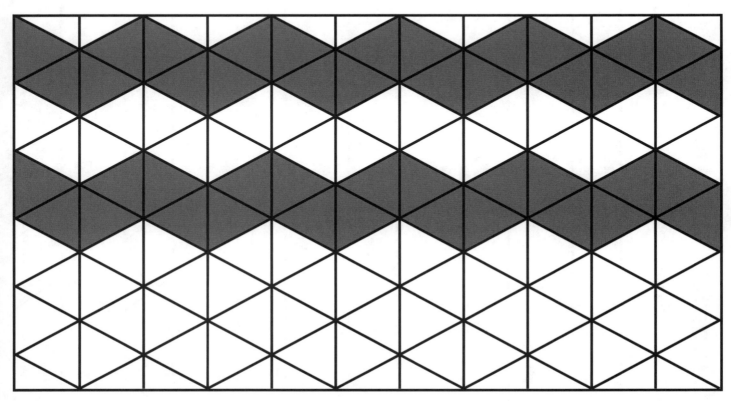

The Square Rose

Name_____

♦ Pick a color. Color one triangle. Then color all the other triangles that are the same size with the same color.

♦ Pick a different color. Color another set of triangles.

♦ Repeat until all are colored.

Stars within Stars

Name_____

- ◆ Pick a color. Color one triangle. Then color all the other triangles having the same size and shape with the same color.
- ◆ Pick a different color. Color another set of triangles.
- ◆ Repeat until all are colored.

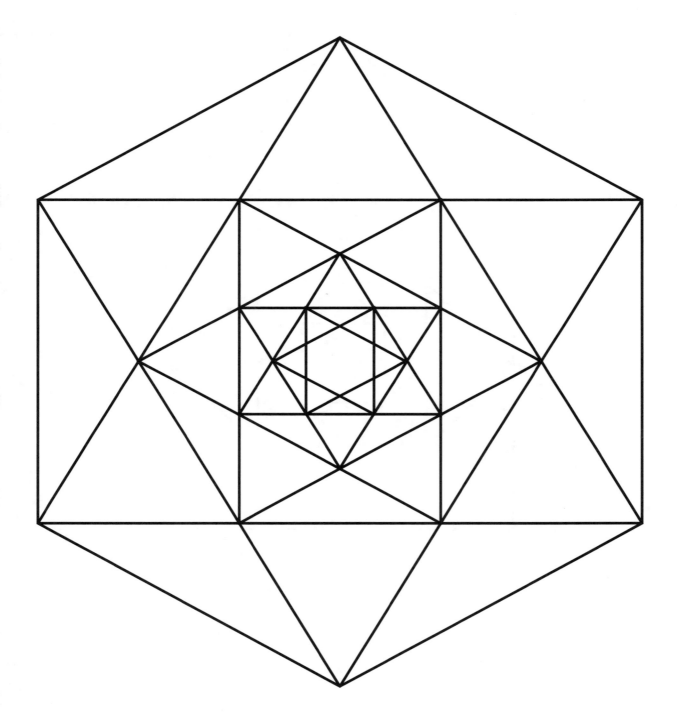

Criss-Cross

Name_____

- ◆ Pick a color. Color one shape. Then color all the other shapes that are the same size the same color.
- ◆ Pick a different color. Color another set of shapes.
- ◆ Repeat until all are colored.

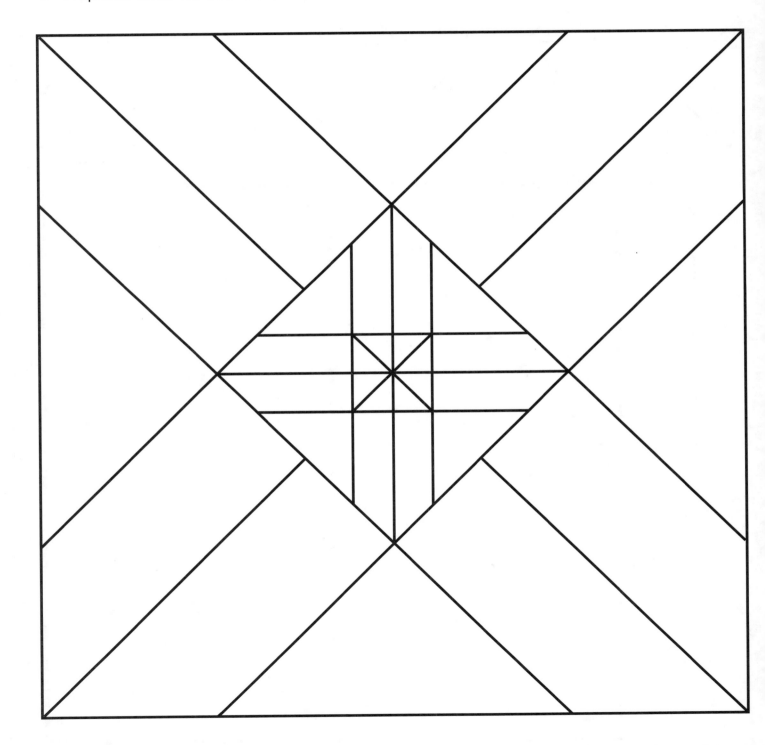

The Folding Square   Name_____

- ♦ Cut out the large square. Fold on each dashed line. Trace the fold lines on the back of the square.
- ♦ Fold flat to make each shape.

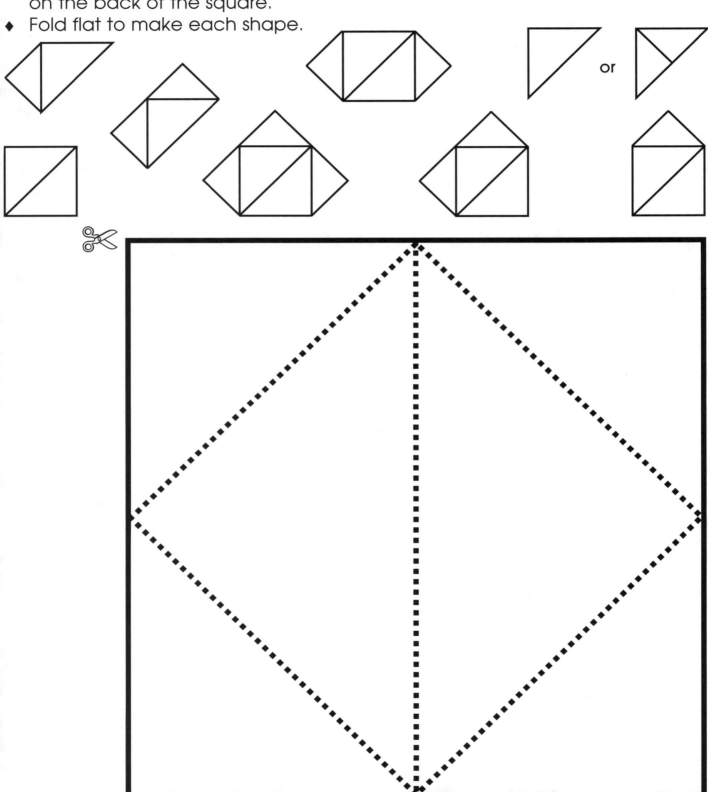

or

Numbers in a Circle   Name_____

♦ Cut out the circle. Also cut on the solid line. Fold on the dashed lines.
  Trace the lines on the back. Write each number in the same place on the back.
♦ Fold flat to make each number combination below.

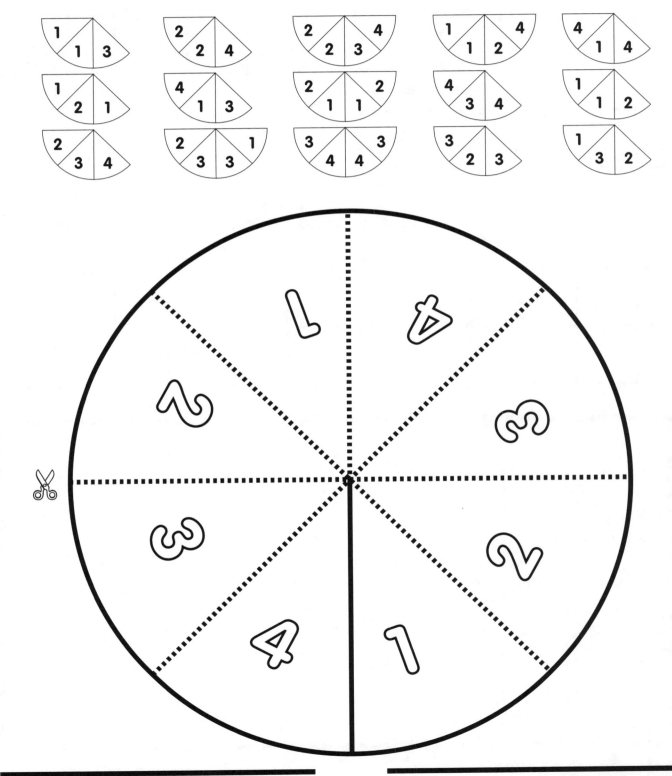

   IF5126 Geometry Grade 2

The Folding Rectangle Name_____

♦ Cut out the rectangle. Also cut on the 3 solid lines. Fold on the dashed lines. Trace the fold lines on the back.

♦ Fold flat to make each shape below.

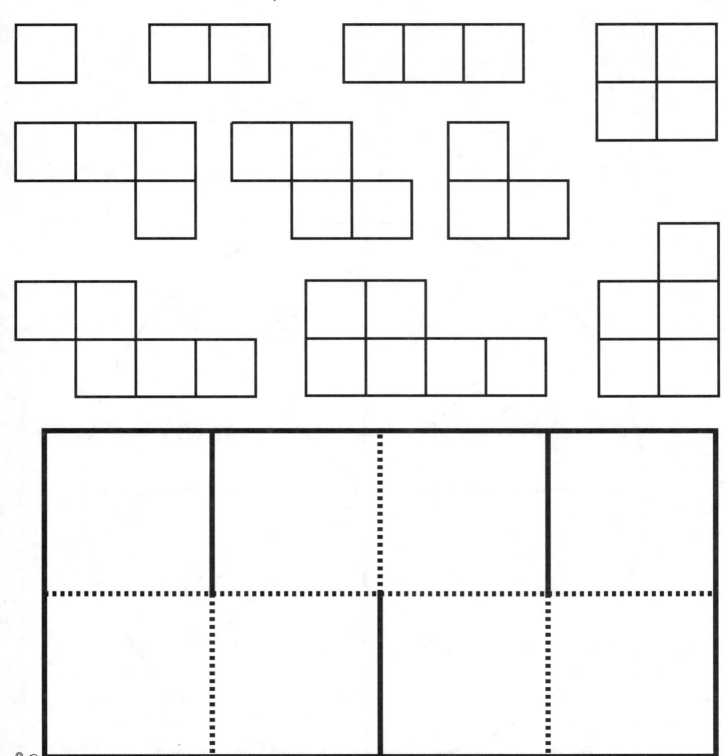

Folded Figures

Name_____

♦ Cut out the rectangle. Cut on the 2 solid lines.
♦ Fold on the dashed lines. Trace the fold lines on the back.
♦ Fold flat to make each shape below.

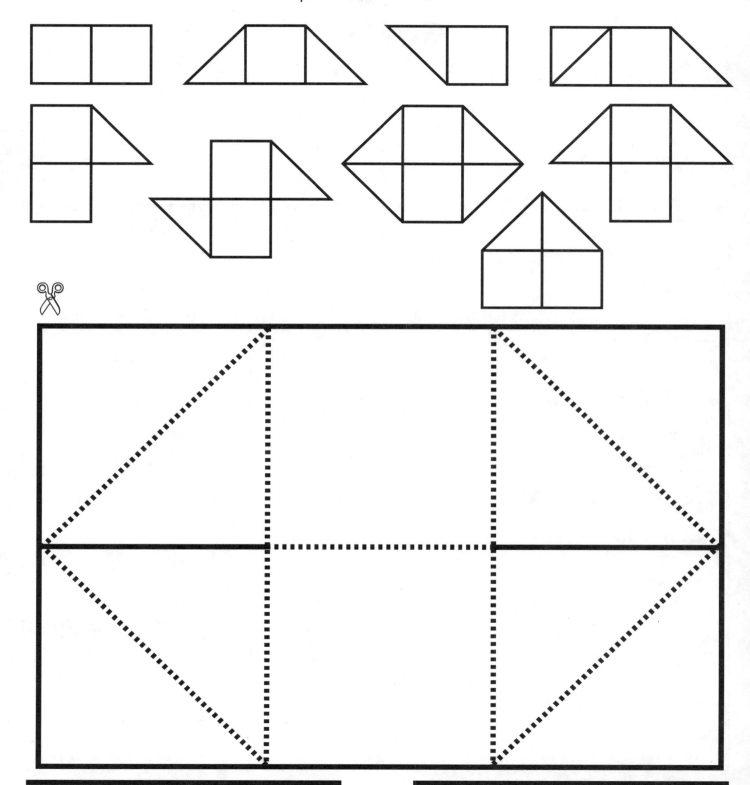

ANSWER KEY
Geometry
Grade 2

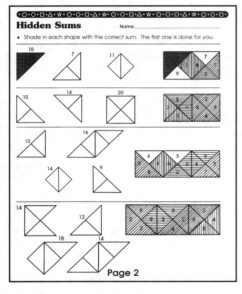

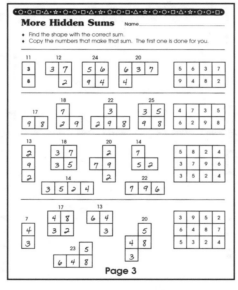

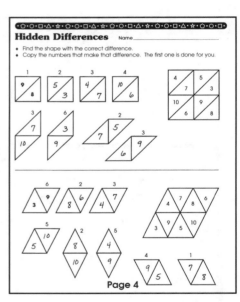

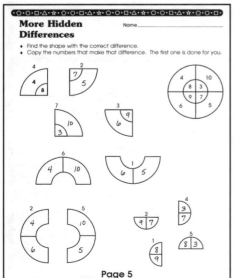

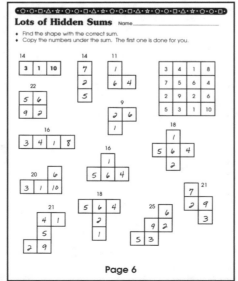

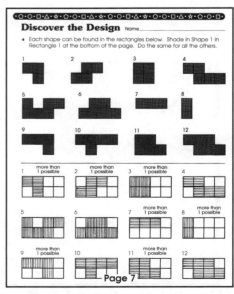

IF5126 Geometry Grade 2

Hidden Shapes   Name_____

♦ Shade each shape in the design below it.

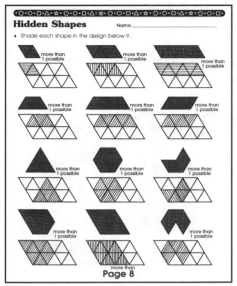

Page 8

Find the Shapes   Name_____

♦ Shade each shape in the design below it.

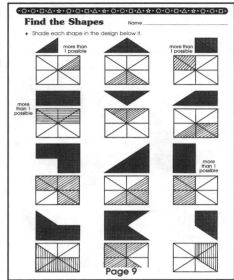

Page 9

Triangle Shapes   Name_____

♦ Shade each shape in the triangle design below. You may need an extra copy of the triangle design.

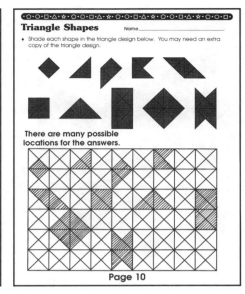

There are many possible locations for the answers.

Page 10

Zigzag Shapes   Name_____

♦ Shade each shape in the design below. You may need an extra copy of the design.

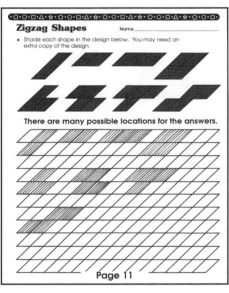

There are many possible locations for the answers.

Page 11

Rectangles in Hiding   Name_____

♦ Shade a different rectangle in each design. Squares do not count.

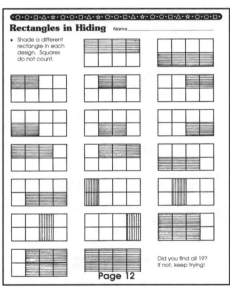

Did you find all 19? If not, keep trying!

Page 12

Four Triangle Shapes   Name_____

♦ Shade 4 triangles in each design to make a different shape.

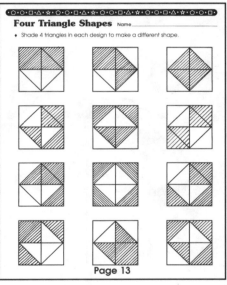

Page 13

Squzzles   Name_____

♦ Cut out all the "A" pieces on the next page.
♦ Put them on Squzzle A so they fit the outline.
♦ Do the same for Squzzles B, C and D.

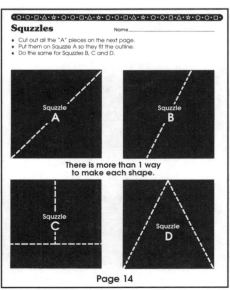

There is more than 1 way to make each shape.

Page 14

Rectuzzle 1   Name_____

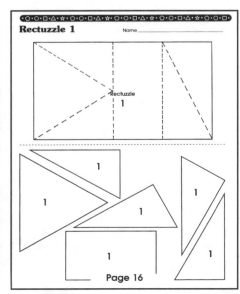

Page 16

More Rectuzzles   Name_____

♦ Cut out the "2" pieces on page 18. Put them on Rectuzzle 2 so they fit the outline. Do the same for Rectuzzles 3, 4 and 5.

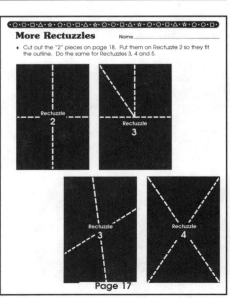

Page 17

© Instructional Fair, Inc.   45   IF5126 Geometry Grade 2

Trianguzzles

Name_____

♦ Cut out all the "A" pieces on the next page. Put them on Trianguzzle A so they fit the outline.
♦ Do the same for Trianguzzles B and C.

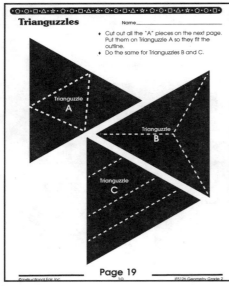

Trianguzzle A
Trianguzzle B
Trianguzzle C

Page 19

© Instructional Fair, Inc.   19   IF5126 Geometry Grade 2

Circle Puzzles

Name_____

♦ Cut out the 4 pieces of the circle. Use them to make each shape.

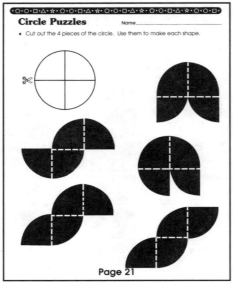

Page 21

XYZ Puzzle

Name_____

♦ Cut out pieces X, Y and Z.
♦ Make each shape below using all 3 pieces.

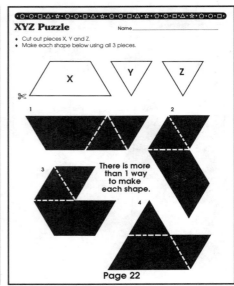

X   Y   Z

1   2

There is more than 1 way to make each shape.

3   4

Page 22

The Two Triangles

Name_____

♦ Cut out the 2 triangles at the bottom of the page.
♦ Make a shape like each below only larger. Use both triangles for each shape. You might have to flip a triangle.

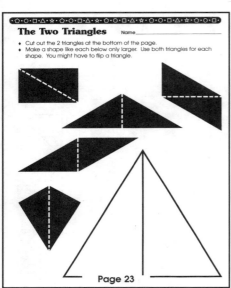

Page 23

Dot Figures

Name_____

♦ Connect some dots in each box using from 1 to 6 lines.
♦ See how many different figures you can make.

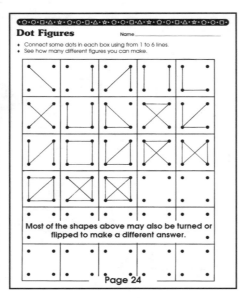

Most of the shapes above may also be turned or flipped to make a different answer.

Page 24

Dots and Shapes

Name_____

Answers may vary.

♦ Connect dots to make each shape described.

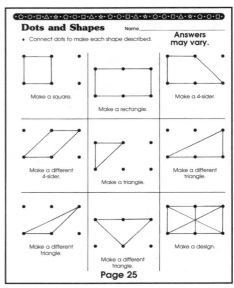

Make a square.

Make a rectangle.

Make a 4-sider.

Make a different 4-sider.

Make a triangle.

Make a different triangle.

Make a different triangle.

Make a different triangle.

Make a design.

Page 25

Hexagon Patterns

Name_____

♦ Shade triangles in each design to make a different shape.

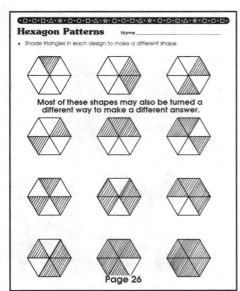

Most of these shapes may also be turned a different way to make a different answer.

Page 26

Triangle Designs

Name_____

♦ Shade triangles in each design to make a different shape.

There are many other possible answers.

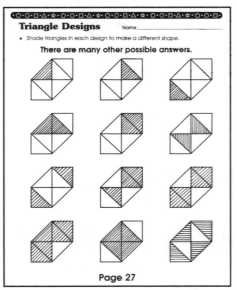

Page 27

Coloring Patterns

Name_____

♦ Use green and blue crayons.
♦ Color the shapes with letters. Then color to keep the pattern going.

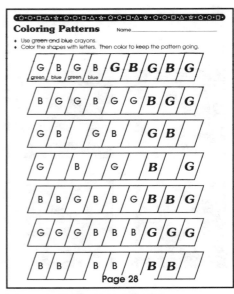

| G | B | G | B | **G** | **B** | **G** | **B** | **G** |

green | blue | green | blue

| B | G | G | B | G | G | **B** | **G** | **G** |

| G | B | | G | B | | **G** | **B** | |

| G | | B | | G | | **B** | | **G** |

| B | B | G | B | B | G | **B** | **B** | **G** |

| G | G | G | B | B | B | **G** | **G** | **G** |

| B | B | | B | B | | **B** | **B** | |

Page 28

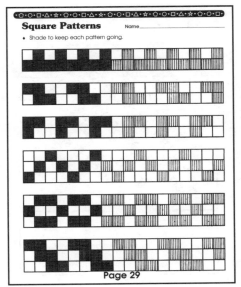

Square Patterns Name_____
* Shade to keep each pattern going.

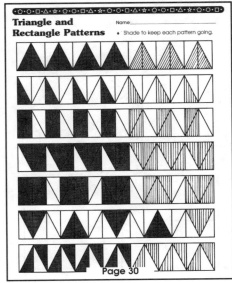

Triangle and Rectangle Patterns Name_____
* Shade to keep each pattern going.

Page 30

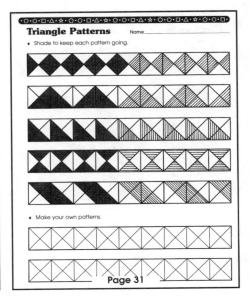

Triangle Patterns Name_____
* Shade to keep each pattern going.

* Make your own patterns.

Page 31

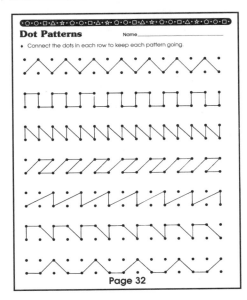

Dot Patterns Name_____
* Connect the dots in each row to keep each pattern going.

Page 32

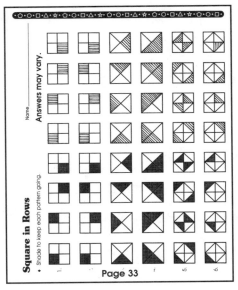

Name_____
Answers may vary.

Square in Rows
* Shade to keep each pattern going.

Page 33

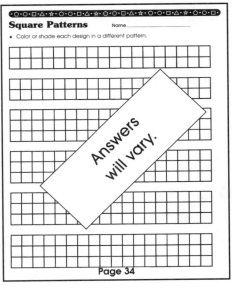

Square Patterns Name_____
* Color or shade each design in a different pattern.

Answers will vary.

Page 34

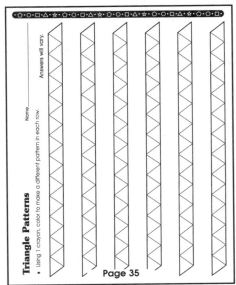

Triangle Patterns
* Using 1 crayon, color to make a different pattern in each row.

Name_____
Answers will vary.

Page 35

Wallpaper Patterns Name_____
* Shade to keep each wallpaper pattern going.

Page 36

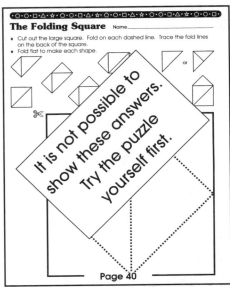

The Folding Square Name_____
* Cut out the large square. Fold on each dashed line. Trace the fold lines on the back of the square.
* Fold flat to make each shape.

It is not possible to show these answers. Try the puzzle yourself first.

Page 40

IF5126 Geometry Grade 2

Numbers in a Circle Name_____

♦ Cut out the circle. Also cut on the solid line. Fold on the dashed lines.
  Trace the lines on the back. Write each number in the same place on the back.
♦ Fold flat to make each number combination below.

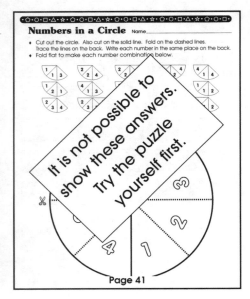

Page 41

The Folding Rectangle Name_____

♦ Cut out the rectangle. Also cut on the 3 solid lines. Fold on the dashed lines.
  Trace the fold lines on the back.
♦ Fold flat to make each shape below.

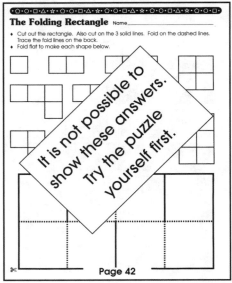

Page 42

Folded Figures Name_____

♦ Cut out the rectangle. Cut on the 2 solid lines.
♦ Fold on the dashed lines. Trace the fold lines on the back.
♦ Fold flat to make each shape below.

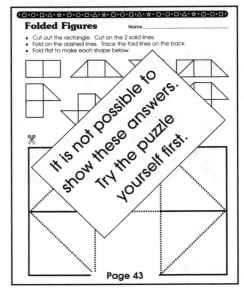

Page 43

It is not possible to show these answers. Try the puzzle yourself first.

It is not possible to show these answers. Try the puzzle yourself first.

It is not possible to show these answers. Try the puzzle yourself first.